Who Stole My Confidence?

7 Rock Solid Steps to
Take Yours Back!

Eileen Strong

Dedicated to Bill, Kristin & Grant....

...the most incredible chapters in my life!

Eileen Strong

Profound thanks to Rebecca Borland, the best editor and friend in the world... Your talents exceed your love and your generosity!

Eileen Strong

Interested in having Eileen speak at your association or organization?

Reach her toll-free at (866) - 531-2387

Eileen@StrongIncentives.com

Look for her next two books coming soon!

"Liars, Tigers, S.O.B.'S!"

Successfully Working With Difficult People

&

"C.H.A.N.G.E.S."

EileenStrong.com   StrongIncentives.com   ConfidenceInCollege.com

Eileen Strong

Eileen Strong

Table Of Contents

Eileen Strong

Eileen Strong

Eileen Strong

Chapter 1: Judgement By Others

It was "dark-thirty" outside.....around 4 a.m.

A flight attendant for P.S.A. airlines; I was checking in 2 hours in advance, as required for a 6 a.m. flight.

Several trips up and down the West coast awaited me that day.

Eileen Strong

I loved this job and I was having fun! Celebrities were frequently on the flights, and the passengers were usually very friendly. My friends and family were envious and proud that I had been selected for this "prestigious" position. Competition was stiff. The uniforms were colorful & short with matching knee high leather boots. Sexy and friendly was the objective. Management wanted us to look a certain way; and we had little choice but to follow it...or else.

That morning I was prompt, coiffed...and in my mind "I was looking good." And then I saw my worst fear.

My supervisor, Barbara Heath.

She sat there next to the scale, holding a tape measure and smiling. I knew my job was in jeopardy, because I already had received a warning about being 5 pounds over my ideal weight according to their charts.

This job required a maximum weight level that was pre-determined by insurance companies and management. Gals were being fired every week, because they had exceeded their weight limit more than 3 times.

Not only did we have to pass rigorous tests by the F.A.A. on a yearly basis, and maintain a high level of positive feedback from passengers and fellow crew members.....BUT also maintain your ideal weight and acceptable thigh measurement.

My self esteem and confidence dropped quickly. What was going to be a great day of work; quickly plummeted into a

Eileen Strong

feeling of angst and apprehension. I felt miserable, and my work day had just begun.

My maximum weight allowed at 5'11" was 150 pounds. This was difficult to keep and maintain. I dreaded stepping onto that scale...but I did.

The numbers went up and up...passed 150. It settled at 154 and I had received another warning. This would be my last one she told me.

At 5'11" and 154, I was quite slender. But I STILL didn't meet THEIR expectations.

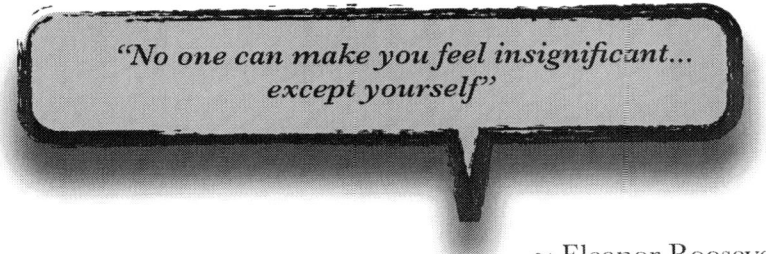

"No one can make you feel insignificant... except yourself"

~ Eleanor Roosevelt

From feeling happy, positive and confident... I felt horrible & had to put on a facade as I faced the passengers all day long.

WHO stole my confidence, that morning?

Was it the presence of my superior? Was it my immediate loss of self esteem, as I looked at myself in the mirror....and hated what I saw?

Eileen Strong

That entire work day, I unfairly compared myself to the other flight attendants and felt fat and unattractive....and only I had allowed myself to feel that way.

I understand that quote now....but I didn't then. I felt miserable, sad and insignificant.

How often have you felt that way?

When you were jeered or not accepted by the popular group in middle school or high school?

When you were lied to by a friend?

When someone stood you up?

When you were not chosen for a job you applied for?

When that phone call never came, when you hoped & prayed that it would?

When you saw a picture of yourself, and hated what the camera showed?

This list can go on and on and on...

Eileen Strong

Take the time now to write down when one of these experiences happened to you.

Be honest how you truly felt when it took place.

Was their anger, confusion, sadness, or self-doubt?

_____

_____

_____

_____

_____

_____

_____

_____

_____

_____

So lets discuss how we can begin to reclaim our confidence....after all, only WE have allowed ourselves to lose it!

Eileen Strong

Chapter 2:   How We Begin To Lose Our Confidence

This is a fact:
Between 3rd grade and 6th grade we have lost over 65% of our self confidence.

When we were young, and I mean young....we were confident and enthusiastic to show off anything and everything about ourselves.

Possibly at age 4, 5 or 6.....

"Mommy, mommy, mommy....look at what I can do......look mommy, watch me do this!"

It could be something as simple as skipping; writing our name; drawing a picture or riding a bike.

The world was our audience. And we wanted to show what we could do.

If we "failed" we simply did it again, and again....and again. Always seeking a new audience or some reinforced

Eileen Strong

attention. We just wanted to show anyone and everyone, what we could do.

Never mind the repercussions, we simply wanted to show off our new "skill."

We did not care what people thought. If it went wrong....we just went on to the next thing.

The freedom of childhood. An eternity of ease and carefree beliefs.

The act of not caring about being judged.

It is such a brief "window" of freedom during our youth. Followed by that life-long "window" of knowing that you are ALWAYS being judged.

Inevitably your "window" begins to close....slowly.

When you attended your first pre-school or Kindergarten class. You remained yourself.

Had fun, made friends...and played carefree.

This lasted for another year or two; and during that time you began to compare yourself to others. And OTHERS were comparing you to them. Everyday in the classroom, the hallways or the playground you were being judged.

Eileen Strong

You were being accepted or rejected...

And if the rejection was frequent, each time it hurt a little more. A malignancy of doubt was being placed in your mind every time.

After a while the "malignancy" spreads. And your self-worth, your self-esteem began to crumble.

Was it the looks you got? Was it the way "they" talked when you walked by.

Was the on again/off again rejection or acceptance?

Any and or all of these motions and emotions took their toll. And you were paying the price. And you WOULD carry it with you.

This self-doubt became like invisible "shackles" around our ankles. We would drag them from experience to experience in our life. After awhile, the emotional burden began to take its toll. You weren't aware of it....it just hovered around our life, our

Eileen Strong

thoughts. And that "ping" of self-doubt would ring again when another negative experience crossed our path.

Yes, life is full of "lessons to be learned"....but lots of these lessons hurt.

So you put on your "game-face" and proceeded on with your day. All the while, these negative emotions were piling up in your sub-conscious. Day after day, month after month...year after year.

After a while you feel you cannot take anymore. This is a red flag...to take a step back and review what is taking place in your life.

Your sub-conscious is constantly protecting you. It is your "guardian angel" reviewing what is taking place. It processes the information, and files it away. And it continues to file similar information till an overload takes place...and you back away...

Unless you have decided to address it...

Eileen Strong

Step 1: Recognize and write down what causes frequent doubt.

Whether it is an event(s) from the past...write it down!

_____

_____

_____

_____

_____

_____

_____

Or a current, "why did I do that"...again?...write it down!

_____

_____

_____

_____

_____

_____

_____

_____

You have to name the emotion at that point. Otherwise you WILL keep on repeating that response. Because we acclimate to a learned response...even if it is not an emotionally healthy one.

We become comfortable with that response, because we don't like change.

Change can be uncomfortable...and usually is. I have frequently told my clients that this is a "broken record" club response.

The response automatically comes up on your "screen." Because you feel safe with that response. You know you need to change the response, but it is uncomfortable. You already know how to respond to that emotion...even though it may not be the healthiest response.

By writing down THAT emotional response you are recognizing it and addressing it. You are beginning the choice to make a change. This recognition allows you to begin reframing this repeated old response...to a brand new positive response!

And this take practice.

And it should take place for the rest of your life!

Writing and reframing how you WANT to respond to an emotional response is critically important in reclaiming a more powerful level of confidence and self-esteem.

This exercise is extremely important. And you must do it.

Eileen Strong

By "writing & releasing" the hidden hurt gets released....sentence by sentence. You must be diligent when you do this.

And the healing will begin and continue. Your roots of a more powerful level of self esteem and confidence will begin to surge... and continue to grow.

Whether you write in a journal for this specific purpose; or simply grab a piece of paper...this healing step is phenomenal! Try it...better yet....do it!

"Never underestimate the power to change yourself"

Eileen Strong

Chapter 3: Choosing To Trust Other People

We were bracing for a crash position.

Circling over Los Angeles....I knew our fuel was being dumped in the Pacific. As the Senior Flight Attendant, it was imperative that I reach the captain to determine whether the passengers should ready for impact.

But, my confidence and trust in the Crew was at a different level. It was challenged...since NO ONE was responding to my emergency calls in the cockpit.

Having flown hundreds of flights, I knew something was wrong. Our plane was circling and circling. I called the cockpit repeatedly; but no one responded. Within moments...I knew why.

Because of no response to my calls, I broke protocol and used the emergency key to open the cockpit door.

Eileen Strong

Stunned, I saw the flight engineer on his hands and knees, manually cranking down the landing gear!

This was bad.

My confidence in the crew "soared and sank" right then. I was trusting them COMPLETELY with my life and all the passengers on board.

As professionals, they were BUSY with the control tower and emergency landing procedures. Working at what they were trained for. Using their confidence and skills to land a 727 airplane full of people!

I reflect now on how Captain "Sully" landed his plane in the Hudson River, and the skill and confidence that it took. Everyone on that historic flight...put their trust in him!

Airline pilots are trained repeatedly to handle these emergencies. They have practiced and prepared for ALL circumstances, and they know exactly what to do......for the sake of the passengers, the crew and themselves.

Just think if you were that well trained to respond to life's unforeseen circumstances!

The inevitable aspects of life would rarely cause us concern or doubt. We would face unexpected upheavals with calmness every time!

But that is not reality.

Eileen Strong

Change is unexpected and comes at us like a truck out of control. And we didn't even hear it coming.

How we adapt to the unexpected, always is a new learning experience.

All the flight attendants on board were trained, for this type of emergency. We precisely followed all the procedures...(along with a lot of prayer!)

Fire trucks were on the runway below. They were ready and prepared for either a catastrophe... or simply another plane coming in for a landing.

We hoped it would be the latter.

Seated, seatbelt secure, and bent forward with my arms encircling my head (known as the "brace for impact" position)....I simply waited that "eternity" for those wheels to touch down and HOLD in place.

5,4,3,2,....1... touchdown.....All of us had the same thought.................. "stay locked,....please don't buckle back up into the wheel well.....stay locked.....stay locked....PLEASE STAY LOCKED!"

And they did!!!

Sirens wailed as the firetrucks followed us down the runway. They were doing their job.

Eileen Strong

We trusted them completely. Always vigilant...always prepared, waiting for the worst... and hoping for the best.

We continued down the runway, with a plane full of passengers...who were taking a deep sigh of relief. Strangers were now hugging each other; followed by applause and cheering. They realized they would be WALKING off this plane.

Mutually our confidence in the captain and his crew were at an all time high!

How many times have you had a renewed sense of confidence in yourself when that contract got signed; or your review was positive and a raise was soon to follow? Or you told someone, how you truly felt about them....(apprehensive of what they may say in return)...but it was positive...and with a sigh of relief....

You felt pretty good about yourself....didn't you?

To be able to "harness" that flow of positive energy would keep you on a daily productive and positive high. Always feeling sure about what you were going to do. Always looking forward to another opportunity because you felt good about what you were capable of doing.

And you ***ARE*** capable of feeling that way.

Eileen Strong

This is where the "power of your mind" comes into play. How you choose to feel about yourself, your attitude & your belief systems. Your attitude truly affects you in a multitude of ways.

Research has supported this mind-set, with many case studies.By choosing to empower your mind-set you are already increasing your level of self confidence.

Books such as "The Power of Positive Thinking" by Norman Vincent Peele and a more current version called "The Secret" are worth owning.

There is a great song called....."I've Got A New Attitude", sung powerfully & soulfully by Patti LaBelle. Please download those incredible lyrics.

Listen truly listen to the words....and crank up the volume!

Do this frequently for your own personal "attitude energizer!"

Soon you'll be dancing and smiling and keeping a "new attitude."

Think of how positive and productive you would be by "cranking up" that song everyday...every morning!

Because you chose a "New Attitude".....full of positive focus and confidence!

Eileen Strong

That power to believe....that power to accept what you want to do; what you want to achieve....must become a concrete belief system within your life. Otherwise it becomes just words. You must focus on this "new attitude"... for it to become an obtainable goal.

Again, think back to your childhood. Remember the story of the little engine, snubbed by the BIG engines. Yet the "little engine" realized the situation and the possibility, that it really could make it up that hill.

Repeatedly the little engine would say to itself......

"I think I can... I think I can... I think I can... "

And of course it DID!

How often did you choose not to do something, simply because you didn't think you could do it?

Asking for that raise.

Calling that certain someone you were attracted to.

Taking that test.

Making that presentation in front of a group of people.

Trying a new sport.

Eileen Strong

Starting and engaging in a conversation with people.

Continuing your education.

This list goes on for your entire life.

It simply will change with the circumstances.

By using positive self talk and setting up a goal chart, each of your challenges and actual "opportunities" can be addressed.

As an adjunct Professor of Marketing & Advertising....I tell my students, always remember that the "brain thinks in pictures." When you want to get a message across, use a picture, along with powerful succinct words whenever possible.

Step 2 : CREATING YOUR GOALS WITH PICTURES

Create a goal chart for yourself, of what you want to achieve. Be realistic on this goal. "Baby-steps" are critically important. Make it realistic... of what you want the outcome to be. If it is weight-loss make it a realistic goal. The group Weight Watchers encourages you to have a 5% goal, and no more! After that achievement, go for your next 5%. And continue your journey from there.

Eileen Strong

Focus on "releasing" your weight, since lost things are usually found. Relationship with food is very powerful. It temporarily meets a need. If the stomach is full, you feel content for the time being. But the hurt can still be there.

Each step you take is moving you forward. Focus on your goal for today. Do what you need to do now, not in the future.

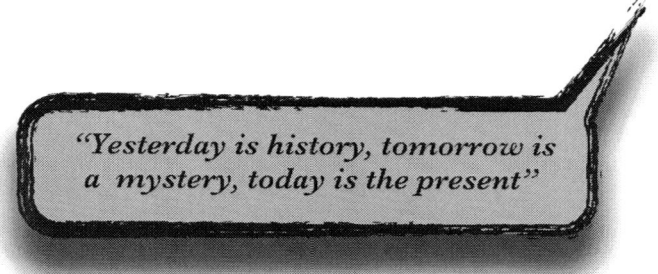

"Yesterday is history, tomorrow is a mystery, today is the present"

Now select one or two pictures achieving that goal. Scan thru magazines, or go on line and find what is an obtainable goal. Do this goal for yourself and no one else. Choose one that will benefit you and not someone else.

Remember this is your journey of life. Focus on you!

Goals can change through out your life. Be flexible and forgiving.

Now draw a line, with a time frame diagramed of what has to be done. Make your dates to achieve these goals applicable for you, and only you!

Eileen Strong

Allow room to be able to write and indicate where you are on this journey.

Look and address it frequently. If changes need to be made, due to current circumstances, that is okay. It's the fact that you have a plan. And that is what counts!

Eileen Strong

There is a recognized acronym for writing down your goals:

S.M.A.R.T.

Specific	*You must be able to specifically state what you want to achieve.*
Measurable	*List what steps need to be accomplished.*
Actions	*State what must you do on a daily basis to achieve this.*
Results	*List the features and benefits of achieving this goal.*
Time	*What is your timeframe to accomplish this in. Make it realistic!*

Use this S.M.A.R.T. guideline as you create your timeline & honor each step.

Eileen Strong

Respect this structure, and your results will be achieved...

Ignore them....and you will flounder...

I speak from first hand experience..!

Eileen Strong

Eileen Strong

Chapter 4: What's Eating At You?

Once you get into this healthy pattern of using goals, soon you will be making great strides in strengthening your confidence personally and professionally.

But sometimes life simply gets in the way though, and puts "chinks in our armor" of confidence. Eventually we are so emotionally bruised we simply believe we just can't go on. We continually use such abusive negative self talk that we fail before even trying.

Eileen Strong

Our relationship with food is masks our emotions frequently. How often have you asked yourself...." Why did I eat that?"

The fact is that we reach for food for a multitude of reasons.

Look at the saga of Kirstie Alley and Oprah and their battle with weight. They openly share it with the media. Over the years, both of them have lost, gained and lost it again. Their journey continues.

Food is simply comforting in so many ways. When you are feeling lonely, upset or out of control.

The term "Comfort Food" is just that. It comforts our emotions, pushes down and covers up what we really are feeling.

Possibly you have heard the sentence......

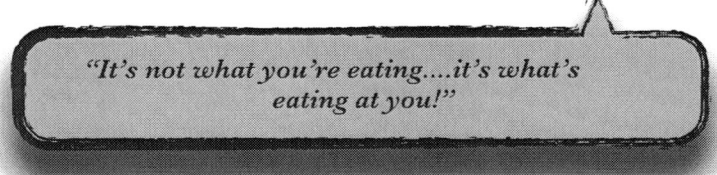

"It's not what you're eating....it's what's eating at you!"

Think about that the next time you reach for the ice cream, cookies, bread, pasta, drive-thru food, second servings of anything....we reach out and temporarily mask what is truly bothering us. We suppress how we truly feel.

Eileen Strong

It is a fact, that when your stomach is full, you temporarily feel safe.

That is the animal instinct that's in us....to feel safe, to simply feel safe.

Regret comes later. When you step on the scale, or look in the mirror naked. Whether the pants don't zip or buttons don't close; no one put that food in our mouths but ourselves.

Whether you are a "closet-eater", (eating when no one is home...or at least in the room you are in)...we eat to suppress our feelings.

And in America we have an abundance of food. Drive-thru's, convenience food, restaurants and outdoor dining spots. All of them promising what we are looking for.

Satisfaction.

Food cannot replace what is bothering you.

The multi-million dollar industry of resolving America's weight problem....is enjoying and profiting from this ongoing emotional angst, that we put ourselves through with each new crisis.

And our confidence is dented again, with each new shopping trip, requiring a larger size....or at least a more flattering mirror!

Eileen Strong

How many sigh's or "Oh-no's" when you stepped on the scale... have YOU experienced?

Learning and understanding that food really is "fuel for your body" not a feast for your emotions. But it usually is "What's eating at you." And that is where the problem lies....within ourselves.

Belonging to a support group, is one of the better ways of addressing emotional eating. The saying "Misery loves company" is very true.

Hearing and sharing with other people that you are not alone. That you are not the only one at night that partakes in mindless eating, is a powerful, healing step.

There are many groups out there too. Weight Watchers, T.O.P.S., (Take Off Pounds Sensibly), Ginny Craig Counselors, etc. Find one or form one yourself. The strength you can find in groups is empowering....and you are worth it.

Eating is emotional. And we are emotional creatures of habit. We frequently treat food as a reward. Remember, it is fuel for our body. Nothing more and nothing less.

I am not stating that creating and enjoying food is wrong. Julia Child reinforced that thru the art of food, you can create, experience and enjoy life in so many more ways.

And she did....in glorious, satiating ways. I think her one word "mantra" was butter. That woman loved and utilized

Eileen Strong

butter in every way possible. And succeeded with each and every new culinary experience.

Moderation is what we clearly need to understand and apply when it comes to food. Doing it alone is difficult. No one needs to be reminded of that. Why not make this journey of acceptance of your body, a healthy one that is nourished, respected, exercised and loved.

Food allows our stomach to be full, therefore feeling "safe." It is just a natural response. And when we feel safe, we function better, we have a stronger sense of confidence. Recognizing that a safe feeling requires you to be tuned in to yourself more closely. Journaling your emotions on a daily basis allows this to take place. You strengthen yourself with each and every written word. And this takes practice and patience, but you are worth the result.

> *"Do everything in moderation, and you will be fine"*

~ *Greek proverb*

Sometimes it's just so difficult to find where you put that moderation. When your emotions are in a "roller-coaster" status, it is difficult to seek that level of healthy moderation. You feel out of control....and quite frankly, don't care. You are living in the moment, and that moment "sucks."

Whether your emotions have been shattered by the"death" of a marriage, friendship, job or actual passing of someone you knew, it takes time to grieve and recognize what has just taken place.

In fact, Dr. Elizabeth Kubler Ross, had made a 5 step recognition program on how one deals with the loss of something. She specifically talks about dealing with physical death, but when you look at her D.A.B.D.A. acronym, you realize that it is applicable to many things in life that are lost, and how profoundly they affect us. Here is her 5 step recognition program...

D.A.B.D.A

Denial	Not accepting what has happened. You are in denial of what happened; have been diagnosed with, or is going to happen to you, and you have little control of the situation. When we feel out of control, we do not feel safe.
Anger	The emotion that surfaces at first when you realize the news. We are angered and annoyed at why this has happened. The irritating fact that this has happened to "me." "C'mon, why me...what did I do to deserve this?"
Bargaining	Wanting to negotiate so that you can change the outcome of impending events. Many people open up "dialogue with God" at this point. Religion begins to grow new roots and compromises are often made...just to make it go away.
Depression	The gravity of what is about to happen pulls you into a mode depression. The length of time that you hover here can vary significantly.
Acceptance	Eventually you realize the inevitable, and accept the impending outcome. You have come to terms with it. You may not agree with it, but you have accepted what is going to happen. Whether it is the loss of life, a job, a marriage, a house, investments....the list goes on.

Eileen Strong

All of us have gone through these steps repeatedly through out our life. Sometimes the 5 steps go past rapidly....other times, they linger painfully and seem to continually create new wounds.

This is where you learn the most. This is where you create stronger levels of confidence, knowing what you are NOW capable of doing. Eventually you feel more in control.

The story of "The Unsinkable Molly Brown" should be brought to mind.

It's a true story, and one that we can all learn from. Her most unique claim to fame is that she survived the sinking of the Titanic, and actually tried to go back and rescue other survivors in the water. She was met with resistance, since surviving passengers were wary that their lifeboat would be capsized by people in the water. Her focus thru out her life was to help other people. And she did. As a philanthropist she gave time and money to help people in need, even when she could have benefited from the help herself. Her drive, her belief system, her will to survive, simply not to give up....simply reinforced her title of being "unsinkable."

Confidence gives you just that! You are so focused on what you are capable of doing, what you are capable of giving....and not looking for anything in return. You believe in yourself. This energy of giving, usually returns back to you in abundance.

Molly Brown looked for little in return, even after the failure of her marriage.

Eileen Strong

She asked for little in support, because she wanted to care for herself...on her terms. Failed marriages can drain you of your confidence. You went into your relationship in good faith, but it fell apart, it collapsed...and you were back to being just you....again. Some where along the way you lost yourself. A divorce is a sign of failure in many ways....yet it recognizes that you have survived! You too, would eventually become "unsinkable!"

The collapse of a relationship is full of emotional based responses, that everyone goes thru dealing with an unpleasant event. This could be physical or psychological....or both. Statistically, those who married in their early 20's have a higher chance of divorce than those who married later in life. The loss of a partner, can create significant damage to your self worth, your self confidence. By focusing on yourself, emotionally, physically and spiritually everyday, you are strong enough to be resilient, and can give back in abundance. You are in control of your own belief systems. This is not a selfish step. This is a step of recognition and belief in yourself ...and it can be life changing.

Step 3: Taking control when feeling out of control

Eileen Strong

Take a pen now and write down a time when you felt out of control. It could be recent, or it could be 10 or 20 years ago.

_____

_____

_____

_____

_____

Remember how you felt then? How do you feel about it now? How do you feel about yourself now?

_____

_____

_____

_____

_____

_____

Writing is a release.

Remember that....writing is a release.

Eileen Strong

By consistently taking the time, even if it is only a few minutes, purge the words from your repetitive thoughts. We tend to rethink, and rehash, something that happened to us.

It becomes a "broken record" and automatic replay in our thoughts. And it is tiring and draining. In its' own abstract way, you feel "safe" with this repeated response. Because the end result is always the same...and the outcome is one you have gotten use to!

Taking the necessary action of writing to release these "why did I do this'...'or why did this happen?"....and rid them from your thoughts.

AND NOW SHRED IT!

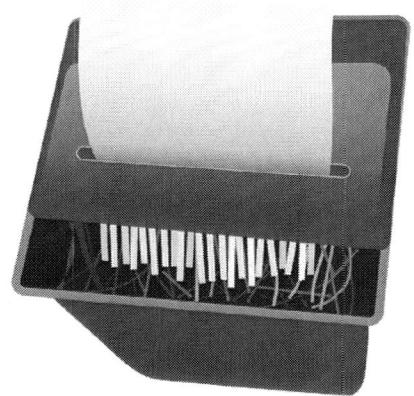

Yes shred it. Physically get rid of the "emotional luggage" that you have carried around too long. You have written to release....now complete the process by physically shredding it from your life.

Eileen Strong

Because the "brain thinks in pictures"...this action of writing, releasing and shredding.....becomes a "mental enema."

You have chosen to rid yourself of all this unnecessary emotional luggage, because it was blocking you and holding you back, from moving forward.
You will emotionally feel lighter and simply better.

You are choosing to live in the present.

Practice this important exercise at least once a month. It is like "cleaning the slate" and allows you to be aware of YOU right here....right now.

Tony Robbins, is a great motivational speaker. His strength is teaching people how to deal and address "their state of mind." He continually pushes you to establish how you are at different points in your life. He inquires "what your state of mind" was and what it is now.

With each new experience we learn. Sometimes positive...sometimes negative. But each new experience does affect our "state of mind."

Your goal is to remain focused on what is the best state to keep yourself in, so that you are productive, positive and confident.

Believe in yourself.

It will be the best investment you will ever make.

Eileen Strong

Chapter 5: Questioning Our Self Worth.

By the time I was 23, I was "damaged goods.

How could so many things have gone so right. ..and then went so wrong?

Why me?

Why did I deserve this?

Why should I feel this way?

Does anybody understand how I feel?

Eileen Strong

Why does life throw us such negative curve balls? From such high's to such a low's... it just doesn't seem fair.

Or so I thought.

By the time I was 17, I was already personally chosen by Eileen Ford of the prestigious Ford Modeling agency in New York City.

I was part of 40 to 50 young models who were competing for recognition at the Bischoff Modeling agency of Milwaukee, Wisconsin. Today was the day that Rosemary Bischoff and visiting Eileen Ford were to pick the model that met their needs...(at least for that day, that point in time.)

We lined up in the room and on the spiraling stairway....and waited to be judged. Non-emotional, just a long appraisal of how you looked. Did YOU have what THEY were looking for?

I stood on that stairway, make-up done, hair just right, black rimmed hat perfectly framing my face.

You could hear the classical music in the background, as over 40 of us simply stood there and posed....and waited.

Waited, as if we were one of the "Christian's in the Coliseum"; waiting for a "life or death", "thumbs-up or thumbs-down" verdict to be placed upon our young lives.

Who stole our confidence there???

We were simply being judged.

Eileen Strong

All of us secretly wanted to be picked. Deep in our private thoughts...it was all that we wanted for that day.

Pick me.....pick me. Please, please, pick me.

And I WAS picked. The only one.

Her sentence was simple. "You....with the hat. Come here."

Slowly, I looked from side to side and realized it was not that gal in front of me nor the gal behind me. Those two professionals had chosen me!

Great for the ego...to say the least.

Like the most popular kid in school saying to you "Want to be my best friend?"

I felt good. No....correction....I felt great.

I was accepted not only by my peers, but I was accepted by someone who I thought was judging me to be worthy of their approval.

How often did you feel temporarily great, because of someone's approval?

Developing a healthier level of self respect, is critically important as we continue this ongoing journey of strengthening our level of self confidence.

Eileen Strong

With the acceptance by these two modeling professionals, I was confident in my skills and newly acquired belief in myself. And it lasted, for awhile.

As I dove into the wild world of professional modeling, I found out what competition truly was. Every casting call, had gorgeous gals in abundance. You would question your validity of being in this field every time you presented yourself and portfolio to an agent. Constant rejection was part of the modeling lifestyle. I struck it rich, when chosen for a 6 page spread in the upscale Town & Country magazine. It was shot at the prestigious La Costa spa in California. To this day it remains a memorable event in my life.

But confidence of this nature is fragile.

Daily we seem to compare ourselves to other people. Always questioning why didn't I do it that way? Why don't I look like them? Why can't I achieve what they did? The comparisons can be endless, as we continually judge ourselves against other people.

The Dove campaign for self esteem in young women, is a positive, powerful program. It continues with their great campaign honoring women of all ages and sizes. Discovering how to feel good about your physical and emotional health is a critical step in solid self acceptance.

As I had mentioned earlier the famous speaker/author Anthony Robbins tell us that this is a "state of mind" that can be addressed, if we choose to change it.

Eileen Strong

Easier said than done.

Previously I had mentioned the "emotional luggage" that we drag from year to year. We find it difficult to change and to leave it behind. These experiences affect how we respond to a multitude of things.

Personally I dragged a lot of negative luggage, since I was a victim of domestic abuse in my early 20's. Statistics have proven that this abuse is at it's highest for women between the ages of 20 - 24. Whether it is physical, emotional or verbal. It is inexcusable!

The first beating left me believing that I had done something wrong to bring this on. What could I do to correct this? Why did this happen to me?

All these questions are asked by victims of abuse every time they suffer another beating. Frequently the beatings are followed by flowers and apologies, or a letter asking for forgiveness. The first few times, this did happen. Then they stopped,... but the beatings didn't.

My level of confidence in myself had simply hit rock bottom.

As it does to this today, for all recipients of domestic abuse.

4 women die everyday from this crime. And it is wrong!

But domestic abuse exists, and I was just another statistic.

Eileen Strong

I hope you never experience it.

But I was going to continue to spiral downward. Out of control. Depressed, angry and sad, because of what happened next.

My mother was terminally ill from cancer. And she would die at the young age of 55.

She never knew what was happening to her only daughter. I carried the burden of abuse AND the crippling burden of watching my mom die at the same time. I was only 22....soon to be 23. Loneliness overwhelmed me.

I wish no one to live thru what I did during those young years of life. Not only did I experience the death of a marriage, but the death of a parent at the same time.

I was alone, sad, scared and depressed. I was miserable, and empty.

I was damaged goods.

We are all products of our environment.

Long term imprinting of our personality takes place between the young ages of 3 and 6 years old. Whether you are exposed to positive, negative or indifferent environments, the core of your belief systems are formed. If you had a parental/ guardian presence supporting you through these formative years, you were fortunate. From an early age you had a feeling of empowerment. You felt good about yourself.

Eileen Strong

Many children do not have that solid and structural building core. Actions or words from a mother, father or family member that deprive you from feeling good about yourself can lead to empowerment being chiseled away. These emotional experiences can be dragged unintentionally, and can affect your resiliency in later years. You are less likely to be capable of fending off any form of abuse. Sadly, abuse affects one in four women through out different stages of life.

No matter what your age, 15 to 95, and you are a victim of abuse, seek help!

Teens should seek help with a school counsellor. Many do not want to reach out for help because they are embarrassed or think that it will NEVER happen again. Sadly, there is an alarming number of young women who are "controlled" by their boyfriends. Demands are made of how you should dress and look for him. Abuse is rampant by these insecure young men, who become threatened, when their girlfriend does not do what they say.

Young women by "nature" frequently want to please who they are with. This is not true of all, but it is quite prevalent. These statistics are overwhelming. Your journey of realizing your self worth starts now. If you cannot go to a school counsellor, contact a parent, friend or relative. Things will not change, until YOU choose to change them. If you knew of a friend being treated this way, what would you tell them?

Eileen Strong

Young women, with or without children, go to the police, a halfway house (day or night) or a place of worship. You will be amazed at the amount of people who are willing to help. But it is up to YOU to ask for it. No one can read your mind.

But they can imagine a situation by your bruises.

When my professor talked to me outside the class room, I lied to him.

With a soft voice, he gently asked "Eileen are you alright? I've seen bruises on you...and I'm concerned."

I ached to tell him. But I didn't have the confidence to tell the truth.

Looking in his eyes, I glibly stated that active tennis playing left me with marks. As a member of the college team, bruises were inevitable. I could tell by his silent response, he didn't believe me. I knew it, and so did he.

His words gave me safe haven. The words were reassuring. I found comfort in them.

But I did nothing about it.

Eileen Strong

"First time a victim....Second time a volunteer."

I hate that sentence...

Eileen Strong

Eileen Strong

Chapter 6 - "Should've, Would've... Could've"

This incredible journey of life is just that. Incredible! No matter how many years you are blessed with; make it a journey of NO excuses.

Those three crippling words have limited us with a litany of why we did or did not do something.

Frequently we preface our reasons for not doing something by saying...

" I would've done it differently, if only I had......................"

"I should've known better? Why did I......................"

" I could've of been so much more if that................................"

Eileen Strong

STEP #4: Eliminating, "Should've, Would've & Could've."

Take the time RIGHT NOW to fill in the following blanks. Do it in pencil, so you can rewrite and reframe how you truly wanted it to turn out. As your confidence grows, you will see your responses becoming more assertive and positive.

Challenge yourself to eliminate these words from your vocabulary. The ease in which we use them as an excuse; or as a reason why we did something, is such an easy exit. You can choose to change this!

Recognize WHY you use those words and WHEN you use them.

Notice when other people are using them and why.

What are they afraid of?

What are they making excuses for?

Start a practice of making a "mental note" ...or by writing down EVERY time you begin a thought or a sentence with those words. You'll be surprised how frequently we let these "excuse" based words into our lives and conversation.

Eileen Strong

Take a few minutes and complete the following three sentences.

"Well, if I had known better I would've" -

_____

_____

_____

_____

_____

"I know I shouldn't have" -

_____

_____

_____

_____

_____

"I could've done better if only" -

_____

_____

_____

_____

_____

The late famous actor, Marlon Brando had a memorable line from the movie "On the Waterfront."

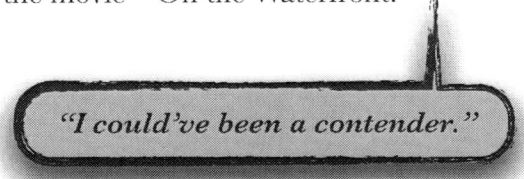

"I could've been a contender."

How often could you have been something, or done something but chose not to follow up or pursue it....anticipating failure or rejection.

The word fear, has been broken into an interesting acronym.

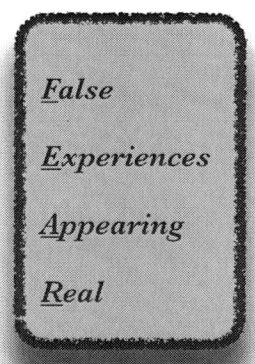

False

Experiences

Appearing

Real

How often has a fear of yours held you back from doing something?

A phone call you had meant to place...but were fearful of the response?

Eileen Strong

A sales call you had to make...but was tired of the rejection?

A class you wanted to attend....but felt you were not smart enough?

A person you wanted to meet....but was fearful of their reaction?

A group you wanted to join...but was fearful of not being accepted?

The list goes on....simply proving that only YOU were holding yourself back!

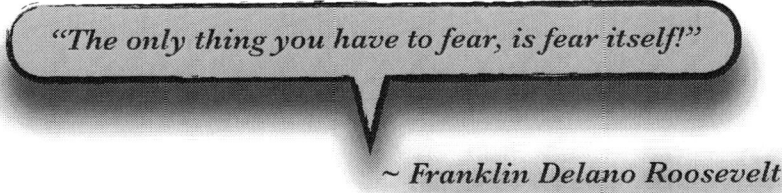

"The only thing you have to fear, is fear itself!"

~ Franklin Delano Roosevelt

This journey of relying on those words, "should've, would've or could've" are easy to fall back on. They give you and "easy out" from focusing on the issue at hand. Simply said they are an excuse for not achieving what you were capable of doing.

The fact is you <u>ARE</u> capable of making a change within your life.

Eileen Strong

What could you have done, if your self-confidence was rock solid?

Begin building a stronger self-confidence by writing down every time you're aware of using those words. Choose not to. You are living in the moment, focused on what YOU are capable of doing at THAT point in time. You feel more sure, clear and aware of you...the real you. Confident in your actions and choices.

It's amazing how we allow ourselves to wallow in what we could, should or would have done.

Challenge yourself to minimize the usage of those words. Focus on what you will, shall and can do. This is your journey, and no one else's. You report only to yourself everyday. So be gentle, kind, honest and loving.

Read that last paragraph again, and understand the depth of it. Because it is true about you. That powerful, wonderful, and incredible being.....YOU!

Eileen Strong

Chapter 7 - Picture Perfect!

It's a fact that the brain thinks in "pictures."

Studies have shown that goals can be achieved, and obstacles overcome by placing pictures of what you want to accomplish.

Eileen Strong

> ## STEP 5: *Visualize how you want to look, act or achieve.*

The "trick" to jumpstarting your response with chosen pictures, is to place them in different places you see infrequently during the day. Want some unique places to display goal pictures?

Try behind the sun-visor of your car; inside a cupboard you open only a few times during the day; in your wallet, or where you hang your coat. You choose where you want to place your goal setting pictures. And then change then every month.

By placing different pictures of a goal you want to achieve in varying places;visually activates your response with more credibility. This technique works!

As you achieve a goal of how you want to look, you feel better about yourself, and your confidence improves.

Putting a picture on the front of your refrigerator, becomes just part of the environment, and the consistency of seeing it so frequently...simply loses its impact. You are no longer aware of that picture. Think of how often you have already done that.

Advertising brochures want you to respond to pictures of clothing that look great. They want you visualize in a positive way, enticing you to buy. Now that America is more than 30% overweight, the catalogues for plus sizes keep growing.

Eileen Strong

A television commercial is a catalyst to motivating you to eat, buy or travel somewhere. A picture is truly worth a "thousand words."

The actress, author Jenny McCarthy states that she drew a diagram of what she was going to accomplish in 2008. Everyday she would look at her visual chart, and reaffirm to herself that she could and would accomplish it.

By early 2009...her book was on shelves AND she appeared on Oprah.

Both of them, just as she had pictured it. During the Vietnam war, P.O.W. (Senator) John McCain along with several other men were imprisoned in what they called "Hotel Hanoi." To pass the long, monotonous days, months and years, they visualized playing games of golf on different courses back in the states; prior to their current internment.

In their mind, they would visualize that some courses were drier, smoother, or more complicated due to recent weather conditions. As they hit the ball with each and every stroke,...their "drives" and "short" game varied.

Imagination was their escape...their freedom.

When released and finally back in the states, their family and friends welcomed them.

And this is the best part.

Eileen Strong

Eventually the opportunity to play golf FOR REAL....had them achieving scores close to par. Even though they had not played for years! Statistically the odds of that happening, are miniscule. (Even regularly playing golfers have a less than 5% chance of shooting par.)

But because they had "played their game" everyday. They were mentally prepared. So focused. So Clear.

Research has shown that athletes who "practice" their game mentally & physically with frequency, actually have exceeded players who participated only physically.

Also athletes who practice a technique called "Eye Movement Desensitization Reprocessing" (E.M.D.R.) reverse winding; can eliminate bad habits they had brought to their game.

As can victims of crime.

Studies have shown that you can "rewind" what happened, and replace it with what you had rather taken place.

Working with a professional who is trained in this technique, can be a life saver, a game saver.

The athlete can "anchor" a positive sound with each performance visualization. Whether they are shooting a basket, swinging a bat, or kicking a ball, or making a touchdown. The frequent repetition of that sound, while completing that shot, swing or kick, etc., "anchors" within your subconscious every time you practice.

Eileen Strong

The power of your mind is incredible!

Theoretically, we use less than 5% of our brain. Just think of the potential within you....waiting for you to tap into it. Your opportunities are endless.

Everyday focus on improving just one thing. Only one. Do this for 30 days straight. And it must be consistent. Whether it is a sport, or an instrument, taking a test or making a presentation. Visualize yourself doing just that one particular thing, and it WILL become a part of your makeup.

I have been professionally involved in the fascinating world of Clinical and Forensic Hypnosis for over 20 years. I have seen thousands of changes made in people's lives, because they changed the way they thought!

Since over 80% of your thoughts come from your subconscious, you really are a product of what you have immersed yourself in.

And you can change what is currently "playing" in your mind.

Choose to change...choose to succeed, is a sentence I have used repeatedly with my clients.

This is YOUR choice to make these changes and no one else. Know and believe that you can change. You can improve your belief system.

Eileen Strong

But it takes practice.

I am sure you have heard the following sentences more than once.

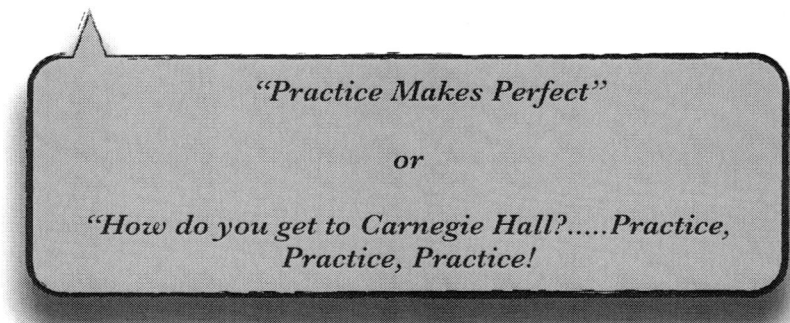

"Practice Makes Perfect"

or

"How do you get to Carnegie Hall?.....Practice, Practice, Practice!

You've heard it before, and it is true. Practice what you feel uncomfortable about; practice how you want to feel, see or believe and soon it will become second nature.

Inevitably, you will feel more comfortable and confident doing it.

Fear of public speaking is the first item on the top ten list of fears people have.

For your information the top ten fears are:

Eileen Strong

1:	**Public Speaking**
2:	**Fear of Flying**
3:	**Heights**
4:	**Claustrophobia**
5:	**Spiders**
6:	**Needles / Getting Shots**
7:	**Death**
8:	**Fear of The Dark**
9:	**Thunder and Lightning**
10:	**Doctors or Dentists**

Since speaking in public is such a crippling experience for most people, let's study a technique that will help you feel more confident the next time you have to make a presentation.

STEP #6 - The Power of Words

Neural Linguistic Programming, also known as N.L.P. has many diverse levels to it. Following is just one aspect of it.

Eileen Strong

Neural	Deals with the power of touch. An incredibly important part to the human beings existence....touch.
Linguistics	Deals with the power of words. Words can hurt and words can heal.
Programming	Means just that. You can positively program yourself to respond to something....naturally.

"Once words are spoken a thousand horses cannot pull them away"

~ Ancient Chinese Proverb

The late Dr. Milton Erickson was the founder of N.L.P.

And he created this "results - oriented" sentence and excercise. When applied correctly it will make an incredible difference in your life.

Eileen Strong

There are a few steps to his technique:

1st:

Take a deep, relaxing breath.

2nd:

Press your right thumb to your index finger. Say the following sentence. * (Listed below, silently or out loud.)

Repeat the sentence with each finger. Say the sentence once, while pressing your thumb to that finger.

Say it and mean it!

Now do this same process with your left hand. Say the entire sentence slowly while pressing only one individual finger to your thumb.

Each time you press a finger, you say the entire sentence again.

Here is the great healing sentence:

"I CHOOSE TO BE IN CONTROL, FEELING CALM & CONFIDENT IS O.K. WITH ME"

Eileen Strong

3rd:
(This exercise takes about 1 minute to complete.)

It's worth the investment of your time. Please say the sentence with credibility. It will have a more positive impact on your belief system.

Lets break apart this powerful sentence and look at the uniqueness of it.

The first part of the sentence addresses a very powerful component of choice. When you state that,

"I CHOOSE TO BE IN CONTROL,"

This is a positive, powerful statement about BEING IN CONTROL and having the capability of choosing to do something.

The middle part of the sentence, focuses on what you are choosing to address:

"FEELING CALM & CONFIDENT"

(this sentence can be adapted to whatever you are choosing to take control of in your life: weight, sleep, stress, test axiety, phobias, etc.)

Eileen Strong

Now look at the last part of the sentence.

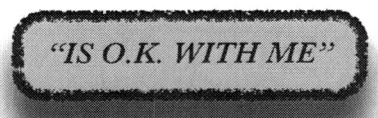

This is a contract of acceptance with yourself and the action you are choosing to do.

Look at it again and understand the importance of this powerful exercise. Realize the benefits you can achieve from it.

"I choose to be in control, feeling calm and confident is o.k. with me."

When you get into a comfortable pattern of doing this DAILY, it will become a "vitamin pill of emotional confidence." By repeating this sentence, you WILL feel more confident and comfortable with new positive empowerment!

Please remember, you MUST say it and believe it.

Your subconscious will honor and act upon it when you do.

Remember... the power of YOUR mind is truly incredible. You can visualize what you want to achieve. Thousands have done it and so can you.

Remember...only you can restructure the way you respond or react to something, through the incredible power of N.L.P.

Only you are controlling the end result.

Eileen Strong

Your choice, your decision.

The steps that you take, will help you achieve what is truly important in your life.

Chapter 8 - Life's Unexpected Bumps

Have you heard of "Murphy's Law?" If something can go wrong - it will!

It seems that whenever life seems to be going smoothly, a "trap door" opens and we fall into a problem that envelopes us completely.

As this journey of life continues, we find ourselves in a myriad of experiences. Some good...some horrific.

The top 5 causes of stress are:

**Death
Divorce
Marriage
Job
Moving**

Eileen Strong

Some people experience all 5 at one time!

If a marriage breaks up, people move and take a new job. Like a chameleon, you adapt to your new circumstances.

Sadly, the marriage statistic of success is still only 50%.

When you walk down the aisle, you never think of that.

Love, hope, and excitement fill your special day. Happiness is inevitable as you look into each others eyes and exchange vows. Your new life is full of promises and dreams. And this is good. For many couples it continues for decades. As it did for my parents.

Let me share with you a part of their love story.

Their given names were Gordon and Beata. And they were in love. Both worked, yet when they came home, he would pin her up against the wall and kiss her as if they had been separated for weeks. What made it endearing was that he would call her "Agnes" and she would call him "Fred." Pet names for each other..... and it was fun watching them engage in this endearment.

Their marriage was solid.

Yes they had a few arguments, but the years they spent together, were full of laughter and love. Two children were produced and raised with strong morals and a focus on education.

Eileen Strong

Sadly, this great relationship would come to an end far sooner than expected.

At the age of 55, my mother was diagnosed with colon/liver cancer. She fought diligently and understood its fatal prognosis. As an Emergency room nurse, she knew what she was up against.

Towards her last month, I vividly remember watching this incredible couple discuss what was happening. I saw my mother sitting on the side of the bed, and softly asking her husband, "Gordy, what am I going to do?"

He was silent as he sat next to his wife of 28 years. Small talk and tears continued between them.

When the doctor walked in and asked to talk to me outside the room, I was not prepared for what I was about to hear. His crippling sentences came out of his mouth in slow motion.

I listened in complete disbelief.

It felt as if the floor had opened up underneath my feet, and I was falling, falling....falling. I took a deep breath when I heard him say, "I am sorry to tell you this, but your mother is going to die. There is nothing we can do. She has only weeks left."

I was devastated and empty.

And I was only 22 years old.

Eileen Strong

The love of my fathers life was being taken away from him. I had to be strong yet somehow "wrap myself around this experience."

Confused, dazed and sad, I simply stood there. Time was irrelevant.

Signe Beata Strong died on July 7, 1972. Three weeks shy of her 56th birthday.

Dad and I buried her urn in a small Norwegian cemetery in Stoughton, Wisconsin.

He never married again. Death affects us all in different ways.

Many relationships crumble when a child dies. Each parent blaming the other for circumstances that they could not control. The hurt becomes unbearable. Words are said that we regret. Our life seems out of control. And we spiral downward into our own personal hell.

Belief systems are challenged and the confidence in yourself to keep going, simply seems to fade.

Their is regret, doubt and anger.

Dr. Joyce Brothers, a recognized psychologist, says that "there is no time frame on grief."

After the loss of her husband, she found solace in "smelling his clothes", simply to linger over his recognizable scent.

Eileen Strong

This journey of life has so many detours. Most of them are never welcomed.

But each and every experience is a life lesson, that you WILL learn from.

You will gain strength and stamina. And hopefully this wisdom will be shared with someone. When least expected you will be reached out to, and you will console and comfort a friend, family member or perfect stranger.

I've said it before, that great lyric sung by the late Jerry Garcia of The Grateful Dead is so powerfully true.

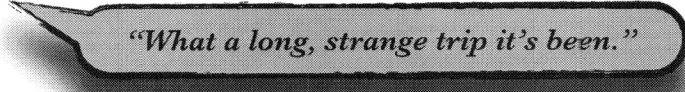

"What a long, strange trip it's been."

After Mom's funeral, my saga continued. I found myself fleeing the verbal and physical abuse of my volatile first marriage. Not only was I groping with the death of a parent but also the "death" of a young relationship.

To this day, I wish no one the double trauma that I experienced at 22 and 23. I was quite young,.... but felt very old and very tired.

How would you have handled it?

Eileen Strong

Within a year I moved back to my parents home in West Allis, Wisconsin and prepared to pick up the "shattered pieces of my life."

Ashamed and depressed, I started putting it back together.

My confidence was gone. One hundred percent, completely gone.

No one had ever gotten a divorce in my family.

None of my relatives, none of my friends, nor anyone in my neighborhood.

I felt like a "loser" and only I had allowed myself to feel that way.

To this day, I hesitate on saying that I got a divorce. I fled so that I could survive.

Staying might have meant that my next beating would be my final and fatal beating.

I chose life.

So with "my tail between my legs" ... I returned home to the bedroom I grew up in.

And started over again.

First things first - complete that Bachelors degree!

Eileen Strong

As my father always said...

> *"Education is something that can never be taken away from you."*

I had completed the Associates, but now it was time to get serious.

I enrolled at the University of Wisconsin - Milwaukee, and took a heavy load of 18 credits.

Plus I worked full time!

I dove in with a frenzy.

Study, work, go to class, take notes, take a test, go to work, study some more. Oh yeah, and get some sleep.

Since my emotional "wounds" were deep and I simply hurt so much; I just wanted to "drown" in the demands of this schedule.

Only I had imposed this sentence upon myself! No jury decided this, just myself.

I felt like a failure.

My mother had died...I couldn't save her. My brief marriage had died....I couldn't save that. I could not save myself from self pity and remorse. And I wallowed.

Eileen Strong

Recognize this sentence?

> *"Obviously, I WAS my own worst enemy. For a while."*

Then I began to gather strength. My intense schedule made sense.

And it worked for me. I didn't want to "come up for air."

Actually, I thrived under the pressure. In fact, I completed my double major Bachelors in Mass Communications and Business in three full semesters plus summer courses thrown in for good measure.

Within 18 months, I headed south to the "Windy city" of Chicago with diplomas in hand.

I had a new attitude and a new plan.

I had regained my confidence.

Eileen was back!

Employment came easily. Soon I was flourishing in the fascinating, creative world of Advertising/Marketing and Sales Promotion. This was to remain a career for over 20 years.

Also, I cautiously fell in love.

Eileen Strong

His name is Bill and I love him to this day. But it was a journey.

We dated for two years and thoroughly enjoyed each others company. Eventually, we moved in together and continued to develop a deep, trusting relationship.

I finally felt safe again. Or so I thought.

After 4 years of a fun-filled, loving relationship, I was given my "pink-slip."

Bill received a promotion and was heading back to his home state of New Jersey. He thought it would be best, if we went our separate ways for a while, and wanted to know if "we could still be friends."

Don't you just love that sentence?

That recognizable "trap-door" opened again. My free-fall of doubt, disbelief and despair returned.

Another broken heart. Another chapter of self-pity. But this time it was different. I felt stronger and more independent. Oh yes, I cried...a lot. I listened to songs of heartache that healed and hurt at the same time. My favorite was by the Fifth Dimension, called "One Less Bell to Answer, One Less Egg to Fry." That song really gave the tear ducts a good workout.

Time passed and my heart healed. I now had become very independent.

Eileen Strong

I had a new attitude and new belief systems.

But I was hesitant. In fact, "skittish."

I was still fragile...underneath this current facade.

Have you ever found yourself in that "state of mind?"

You question your self worth.

Being rejected by another person erodes our self confidence. And this can happen at ANY stage of your life. No matter what decade of life you are in. Each broken relationship seems to hurt every time. Inevitably, you question your self worth again. But as a result, an inner strength develops within you. This healing process benefits you in the long run. And the stronger you are, the more confident you become.

It actually becomes a badge of courage. Each broken heart, strengthens you as you mend.

And you wear those invisible medals with pride. Whether you consider these emotional treks, a waste of pain-filled times or a unique life experience, it's your choice.

Make it a lesson that you learn from. Then go onto your next "chapter" in life.

STEP # 7 - JOINING OR CREATING A GROUP

Eileen Strong

Some of you have probably heard the saying "Misery Loves Company." You commiserate with someone and share stories of what happened, and in return they tell you theirs.

This is good.

You are verbally and emotionally releasing an experience that affected you in a profound way. This is a healing catharsis. By sharing and expressing your feelings you are letting go of a scenario that continually replays in your mind.

Remember that *"broken record club"* I talked about in Chapter 4?

Well lets begin the next healing step and take yourself to abundant confidence and success.

Begin a search for compatibility. Start with the internet and look for interesting groups that are online or have local groups relating to your most prevalent issues. Possibly you can reach out to a faith based group.

So many of us flounder with emotional turmoil in our life. It seems to be the younger you are... sometimes temporary decisions are made, that have permanent solutions.

If you feel you have lost your reason for living Please seek professional help.

Eileen Strong

Be cautious when online. Read and review as much as possible about any social networking groups. Usually, you'll find one or two that relate comfortably to your needs. For some people, keeping a "physical distance" by joining an online group makes them feel safer. Again, this is your choice.

If "one on one" counseling with a trained therapist is temporarily best, do that. Or if a group gathering is best, do that.

Consider possibly creating your own group. Schedule meetings that gather with frequency (at least once a month). Talk therapy is very healing. Sharing with other people and finding how they addressed an issue, helps you realize that you are not alone and someone else has already been on a similar journey.

The power of talking about an issue in a "healthy" environment can be a cathartic release. But learn how to communicate effectively.

As Dr. John Gray, author of "Men Are From Mars, Women Are From Venus", says we simply communicate differently.

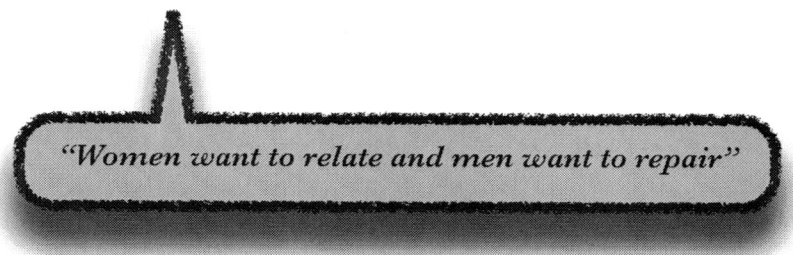

"Women want to relate and men want to repair"

Eileen Strong

Think about the power of his words. Men see an issue at hand and want to address it directly and look for a solution to the problem. Women do it much more circuitously. The end result is the same. It is just done in a different manner.

Whether you find or create a group, become an active part in it. Don't sit on the sidelines. Engage, listen, share, vent, and talk. Then listen some more. Remember you have two ears and one mouth.

Do the math.

Many small businesses form "MasterMind" groups so that they can exchange information, problems and goals with each other. Usually this synergy of energy proves to be an asset, to all who take part in it.

And that is how you should approach the "life and length" of your group. What do you want to get from it, and what can you give in return? Could this be a short term group or could this be the "beginning of a beautiful friendship" as Humphrey Bogart said at the end of his famous movie "Casablanca."

The choice is yours, as it is with every aspect of your life...

Eileen Strong

So lets recap these great 7 steps that can truly make a difference.

Step 1:	*Recognize Your Self Doubt and Loss of Confidence.*
Step 2:	*Create Your S.M.A.R.T. Goals*
Step 3:	*The Power of Writing, Releasing & Shredding.*
Step 4:	*Eliminate "Should've, Would've, & Could've."*
Step 5:	*Picture Perfect....Visualize Your Goal.*
Step 6:	*The Incredible Power of Words. The Power of N.L.P.*
Step 7:	*Group Therapy*

Eileen Strong

To complete a puzzle, you must put ALL of the pieces in the right place.

Thus, you must honor all 7 of the steps you have read, lingered over and learned from. As a result, you WILL take back your self confidence.

I did....and so can you! There is a famous sentence that makes you think about change.

> *"If you always do what you have always done, you will always get, what you have always gotten!"*

You CAN choose to change, and better yet you can choose to succeed!

Make the right choice for you. It will be your best investment.

The "return" will be priceless!

A rock solid confident person, who savors life. and lives it to the fullest.

CONGRATULATIONS!

Eileen Strong

Eileen Strong wearing the
"Ta Da Cape of Confidence"
(Property of Author & Speaker Loretta LaRouche)

About Eileen Strong:

A transplanted midwest Wisconsin gal, now living on the "Jersey Shore." She is loving, and living life to the fullest as wife, mother, and great friend. She is a professional speaker, trainer, adjunct professor of advertising and marketing, and presentation skills expert. Helping people reclaim and regain their confidence to a new, more powerful level, is her objective and goal.

Notes for a
book-club
work book:

#1: Discuss and share, your earliest memories of not feeling sure about yourself in elementary school, middle school, high school or college.

_____

_____

_____

_____

_____

_____

_____

_____

_____

_____

_____

_____

_____

_____

_____

_____

_____

_____

_____

_____

_____

***#2: Discuss and share how you felt when
someone you trusted, let you down.***

_____

_____

_____

_____

_____

_____

_____

_____

_____

_____

_____

_____

_____

_____

_____

_____

_____

_____

#3 *Was this a trusted personal friend, or was it a family member or a co-worker who said or did something to affect the way you felt about yourself? Discuss how each of these possible friend, family or work associations have affected your self esteem.*

_____

_____

_____

_____

_____

_____

_____

_____

_____

_____

_____

_____

_____

_____

_____

_____

#4: How has a relationship affected your life and self-confidence, when difficult times were prevalent? Your journeys in life, can sometimes be at the "top of the hill" or at the "bottom of a valley." How have you felt about yourself and the relevance of that person in your life?

_____

_____

_____

_____

_____

_____

_____

_____

_____

_____

_____

_____

_____

_____

_____

_____

_____

_____

#5: When your self-esteem and confidence are strong, what are some different feelings you have about yourself? How do they differ when you are experiencing self doubt?

_____

_____

_____

_____

_____

_____

_____

_____

_____

_____

_____

_____

_____

_____

_____

_____

_____

_____

_____

Collectively have your group work through all 7 steps together. Share with each other your feelings as you engage with each step. Then celebrate the confident, positive and focused new you, on this incredible new journey in your life.

> No matter how long the journey, it always begins with the first step!"

~ Author Unknown

Authors Additional notes:

It is important that you pick up this book again in 6 months to no more than a year. Discover how your level of confidence has grown and changed. Please give time for this journey to take place. Life can change in so many ways, even within a very short period of time.

Recognize and embrace each and every challenge and change that comes your way. Yes they can be uncomfortable and even hurtful, but as you grow, so will your confidence.

This is an ongoing process, and you must spread your wings to feel the lift and accept each new chapter in YOUR life. This investment in yourself is worth the tears, fears, time and effort you have put into it.

Dr. Barbara Becker Holstein -

Author of: "I'm a girl, I'm smart & I know everything" &
"Secrets - I'll tell you my secret, if you tell me yours....maybe."

"As a positive psychologist I am always searching for self-help books that are on target psychologically, uplifting and filled with tips that really make sense. This book fulfills all of the above requirements! It is emotionally sound, based on best principles and mental hygiene. It is made even more powerful by personal stories, interspersed with fundamental principals of positive thinking and goal setting. And the book leaves the reader ready to build or rebuild their own life, hopeful and oriented to positive outcome. I highly recommend "Who Stole My Confidence"! Read it yourself and give it as a gift to others. What a great book Eileen!"

Pastor Joseph Gratzel -

First Baptist Church, Manasquan, New Jersey

" I frequently work with people who are dealing with life's conflicts." Who Stole My Confidence" is a poignant journey of discovering how to reclaim yourself. It offers steps that are powerfully helpful, pragmatic and honest. I know they will make a difference in many peoples lives."

Bette Wary -

Retired High School Teacher

" What a great book for a book club! It offers discussions and dialogue that everyone can learn from. You offer insight and steps that many people can learn from. Great job Eileen, I really loved your book!"

Lynne Groves -

Professional Sales & Marketing Trainer

" You are one incredible gal! I loved every page of this book. It can be successfully used at any age of life. Can't wait for your next book. Thank you Eileen!"

Notes to myself on this journey
of growing my self confidence:

_____

_____

_____

_____

_____

_____

_____

_____

_____

_____

_____

_____

_____

_____

_____

_____

_____

_____